12°°

S0-DTC-621

27
365
365
365
365
1̶7̶ 8̶10
-365
1095

SNATCHED
AWAY!

SNATCHED AWAY!

SNATCHED AWAY!

CHUCK SMITH

The Word For Today
Costa Mesa, California

Library of Congress Cataloging in Publication Data

Smith, Chuck.
    Snatched away!

    1. Rapture (Christian eschatology)   2. Tribulation (Christian eschatology)   3. Second Advent.   4. Bible—Prophecies.   I. Title.
BT887.S6   236'.9   76-26645
ISBN 0-936728-06-X (previously ISBN 0-89337-004-5)

CONTENTS

SNATCHED AWAY!

INTRODUCTION

It is essential that Jesus Christ comes again. It is essential for the survival of this old planet earth. We won't make it if He doesn't come again. Man can't survive. We're admitting now that the complexities of society are greater than man can handle. We thought for a long time that we could control the economy. We're finding out that we can't control the economy. We thought that we could control food production. We're finding that we can't control food production. We thought that we could handle the complexities of our society, but it's becoming so complex that government is almost throwing up its hands. It seems the only solution our government is trying is to throw money at any problem, and hope that it'll go away.

We are really not facing the issues. We're really not dealing with the problems that are compounding faster than we can handle or adjust to.

The Bible speaks of distress of nations with perplexities. The word "perplexities" in Greek means "no way out"—how descriptive of the current national scene!

3

It's essential for Jesus to come again—not only to save man, but to fulfill all the prophecies. In His first coming there were over 300 prophecies that were fulfilled. For His second coming there are many prophecies yet to be fulfilled. It is essential that He comes again to complete the prophetic picture and to fulfill the remaining prophecies. And Jesus is coming again.

SNATCHED AWAY!

Lord
My soul is thirsting
for a Blessing to day

Let the spirit fall
around —

For

Lord my soul is
thirsting and I want
a refreshing —
Lord my soul is
thirsting & I need a
fresh Touch

grant me a blessing
To day
To day

Chapter 1

What's It All About?

The rapture refers to that event where Jesus Christ snatches His Church out of this world. It shall happen suddenly without any notice. "For the Lord himself shall descend from heaven with a shout, with the voice of the archangel, and with the trump of God: and the dead in Christ shall rise first: then we which are alive and remain will be caught up together with them in the clouds, to meet the Lord in the air: and so shall we ever be with the Lord."[1]

There is a difference between the rapture of the Church and the second coming of Jesus Christ, and it's important that we clearly distinguish between these two events.

At the rapture of the Church Jesus is coming *for* His saints. The Lord doesn't come back to the earth at this time. We, the Church, will be with the Lord, though, and that's the important thing. But we won't be with the Lord in heaven forever. We'll be with the Lord in heaven for a 7-year period during which time the earth will experience what's known as the Great Tribulation, when the judgment of God is being poured out upon the earth (*see* Appendix).

At the second coming of Christ, Jesus will be coming *with* His Church. We'll be returning with Jesus Christ at His second coming. The Scripture said, "Behold, the Lord cometh with ten thousands of his saints."[2] Paul said, "When Christ, who is our life, shall appear, then shall we also appear with him in glory."[3] Many Scriptures refer to the coming of Christ with the Church, or with the great throng and the great multitude, to set up His kingdom.

Where?

Now, there are some people who would ridicule the idea or concept of the rapture of the Church. They declare that the word "rapture" isn't even found in the Bible. It all depends on what bible you're reading. Paul said, "Then we which are alive and remain shall be caught up."[4] The Greek word *harpazo* is very forceful; it's "taken hold of by the collar and snatched away violently." In English we didn't have any one word which could translate the Greek word.

Actually, the Greek language is so much richer and fuller than the English. I was studying the word "take" in the Greek and found that there were no less than 35 different Greek words for our English word

8

"take." You can imagine the difficulty of trying to translate Greek into English when there are 35 different Greek words for one English word. It's whether you "take it lightly," or you "take it hard," or you "take it up," or you "take it down," etc. They have a different Greek word for all these. We have to add our English adjectives or adverbs to describe it. Yet, in the Greek they have a different word to describe all these actions.

The Greek *harpazo*, which is "to snatch away violently or by force," was translated as "caught up." The Latin equivalent is the word *raptus* which is in the Latin Vulgate, one of the oldest manuscripts in existence. When a person says that the word "rapture" isn't in the Bible, it's just not in the King James. But if you're talking about the Latin Vulgate, it's there. The word "rapture" in English is a transliteration of the Latin word *raptus*.

Likewise, you'll not find the word "millennium" in the New Testament or in the Bible. "Millennium" is a Latin word meaning "a thousand years." Yet, you'll find in your English Bible the reference to "thousand year" reign of Christ which, again, in the Latin Vulgate is *mille annum*. Because the word "rapture" doesn't appear in your English text doesn't at all negate the truth of the rapture of the Church.

And so, "The Lord himself shall descend

from heaven with a shout, with the voice of the archangel, and with the trump of God: and the dead in Christ shall rise first: then we which are alive and remain shall be snatched away by force together with them in the clouds, to meet the Lord in the air: and so shall we ever be with the Lord."[1]

Who?

The Jehovah's Witnesses laugh at this concept and say: "You think you're going to be forever in heaven. I don't want to be forever in heaven. I don't want to be on a cloud playing a harp!" They make light of the heavenly scene. I don't know whether I want to be on a cloud playing a harp and I don't know where the Scripture says I'm going to. But it does say I'm going to be forever with the Lord, and that's where I want to be.

When He's in heaven, I'll be in heaven. When He comes back to earth, I'll come back with Him. When the earth and heaven are taken away, and there's a new heaven and a new earth, I'm going to be there with the Lord. When He inhabits that portion of the new universe—wherever it is—that's where I'm going to be, too. For I'm going to forever be with my Lord. That's the promise for which we rejoice. And whenever I'm with Him, that will be heaven!

Paul said, "Behold, I show you a mystery; we shall not all sleep, but we shall all be changed [metamorphosis, a change of body], in a moment, in the twinkling of an eye."[5] It doesn't say "wink" of an eye—it says "twinkling." You can *twinkle* your eye ten times while you *wink* it once. The rapture will happen much faster than the wink of an eye. Suddenly, you're going to be gathered together with all the Church and with the saints that have gone before, and forever be with our Lord.

John writing to the Church said, "Beloved, now are we the sons of God, and it doth not yet appear what we shall be: but we know that, when he shall appear, we shall be like him; for we shall see him as he is."[6] Jesus is going to appear one of these days, and I'm going to be changed in a moment, in the twinkling of an eye, and I'm going to be just like Him. "For our citizenship is in heaven; from whence also we look for the Saviour, the Lord Jesus Christ: Who shall change our vile body, that it may be fashioned like unto his glorious image."[7] Describing the metamorphosis Paul wrote to Corinth, "For this corruption must put on incorruption, and this mortal must put on immortality."[8]

One of these days very soon there's going to be some beautiful changes made. I'm going to get a whole new body direct from God, geared and equipped for the universe. No longer earthbound, but a body that has been adapted to the environmental conditions of the universe. "As we have borne the image of the earthly, we shall also bear the image of the heavenly."[9]

I'm made up of 14 elements that compose the dust of the earth. But I'm going to have a new body which will be made up of the elements that compose God's eternal kingdom. I don't know what they are yet. I'll find out one of these days. I'm living in a perishing tent, but I'm going to move into an incorruptible house—one that is not defiled and fades not away, that has been reserved in heaven for me as I'm being kept by the power of God through faith.

You may be saying: "That sounds neat! As soon as I hear the trumpet sound I'm going to fall on my knees and say, 'Okay, God—quick, save me!' I'm just going to have my fun and everything else until the trumpet sounds and then I'll squeeze in!" That concept stems from a couple of Satan's lies.

The first one is that being a Christian isn't fun. That's a lie. The most glorious life in the world is the life lived with Jesus Christ. The second lie is that you'll have a chance to squeeze in at the last moment. The rapture will happen so fast that, just like in a car accident, you really won't know what hit you until it's all over.

All of a sudden you're going to take a breath and there's no smog. The whole thing is going to be opened up in such glory, such beauty, such love, such joy you've never felt. And then the realization—it happened!

12

Wow! That's the kind of exhilarated feeling I'm looking forward to when Jesus comes.

There are others who'll have an opposite emotion. All of a sudden they'll be looking for their Christian friends, but all they'll find is a big empty tent or building. And then the realization is going to take place—it happened. But there won't be joy, there won't be exhilaration. There won't be a thrill, there won't be love. There won't be excitement. There'll be a horrible consciousness of "I'm too late!"

When?

Jesus said, "But of that day and hour knoweth no man, no, not the angels of heaven, but my Father only."[10] What day or hour? The day or the hour of His second coming? No. I believe that man will be able to tell the very day the second coming of Jesus Christ will take place, but not the rapture of the Church.

Daniel said that from the time the abomination of desolation is set up until the end shall be 1290 days.[11] When those that are upon the earth see the Antichrist set up his image in the temple (the abomination of desolation), they can start counting, and in 1290 days the end will come. Blessed is he who waits for the 1335th day which will actually bring the establishing of the kingdom of Christ over the earth. That interim time between the second coming and the establishment of His kingdom is His judg-

13

ment of the nations. But the very day of the end is predicted in the Scriptures by Daniel, and the marking point of it is the day that the Antichrist sets up his image in the holy place.

Then what's Jesus talking about, "But of that day and hour knows no man"? He's talking about the rapture of the Church.

Jesus went on to explain with other parables. He said, "As the days of Noah were, so shall also the coming of the Son of man be."[12] Actually, in the days of Noah they were eating and drinking, they were going on with business as usual and, suddenly, the flood came and took them away. Jesus was saying that we'll be going on with business as usual and, suddenly, the Lord is going to come and take us away.

Jesus said that two will be going forth into the field and one will be taken and the other left. Two will be grinding at the mill, one will be taken, the other left. Two will be sleeping in a bed, one will be taken and the other left.[13] Isn't that interesting? Jesus showed that He knew the world was round. You go out into the field in the morning, you're grinding at the mill in the evening, and you sleep at night. Simultaneously, all over the world, some will be sleeping, some will be going out in the morning, and some will be gathering together in the evening time. From all over the world at once the Lord is going to take His Church right out of the earth. No matter what you're doing!

I don't believe the Lord will give the Church any special forewarning. To declare some date or some hour would be an unscriptural presumption. If we say we know the day and the hour, we're boasting to superior knowledge than what Christ had when He was upon the earth. I'm opposed to all date-setting for the time of this event. I don't believe that God will in these last days give us any special warning. I don't believe that, suddenly, some angel is going to appear on a Sunday morning and say: "Get ready, folks! Next Saturday at 2!" No, the Lord is suddenly, at any moment, going to snatch us all out. You won't even realize what's happened—nor will the world—until it's all over, and we're gathered together with the Lord rejoicing in His grace.

However, even though we don't know the day or the hour, Paul said: "But of the times and the seasons, brethren, you have no need that I write unto you. For yourselves know perfectly that the day of the Lord so cometh as a thief in the night. For when they shall say, Peace and safety; then comes sudden destruction . . . But ye, brethren, are not in darkness, that that day should overtake you as a thief."[14] The Bible is saying that it shouldn't come to you as a surprise—"that day" shouldn't overtake you as a thief. Why? Because God has given to us the signs and the evidences that would precede the coming of Jesus Christ.

How?

At this point you may be asking, "How do you become a member of the true Church?" It's not something that you can join. You've got to be born into it. Born again by the Spirit of God. Jesus said, "Marvel not that I said unto thee, Ye must be born again."[15] How can a man be born again? Can you enter the second time in your mother's womb and be born? No. That which is born of flesh is flesh. You need a spiritual birth. That which is born of the Spirit is spirit. How? "As Moses lifted up the serpent in the wilderness, even so must the Son of Man be lifted up: that whosoever **believeth** in Him should not perish, but have eternal life."[16] Believing on Jesus Christ is the only way to be born again. "For God so loved the world, that He gave His only begotten son, that whosoever believeth in Him should not perish, but have everlasting life."[17] That's how. Just believing in Jesus Christ and turning your life over to Him.

NOTES

Chapter 2

The Fig Tree

One of the greatest signs in the world today that Jesus is coming again soon is the rebirth of the nation Israel.

For years Bible scholars have been looking for the reestablishment of the nation Israel. They've been declaring that God was going to bring the people back into their land. The skeptics used to really laugh at the Bible believers and their claim that a nation would be born out of the past. It had never happened in history. To say that this nation could be established again was just incredible. But Bible scholars kept affirming and looking forward to it. Back at the turn of the century they were still laughing at the Bible scholars because there were fewer than 10,000 Jews in all the land of Palestine. But let me tell you something, they're not laughing anymore.

God has fulfilled His word. A miracle has taken place and a nation has been born. God has reestablished the nation Israel among the family of nations in the earth. They're in their own land. They have their own government. God has fulfilled His promise even as He said He would.

The gathering again of Israel in the Scripture was always given in the context of being in the last days. In Ezekiel 38 God said that in the latter days He would gather them back again into the land from all the nations from whence He had driven them, and they'd be dwelling there within their cities. God speaks of it as in the last days. Twice He makes that reference in Ezekiel 38.[1]

In Psalm 102 the Psalmist declared, "When the LORD shall build up Zion, he shall appear in his glory."[2] That's why the orthodox Jews today are looking for their Messiah. The Lord is building up Zion and they are now looking for their Messiah to appear in His glory. We are too. We're waiting for the coming of our great God and Saviour Jesus Christ.

The return of the Jews to Palestine and the reestablishment of the nation Israel was to the Bible scholar and to the Church a warning and a sign from God that the end was at hand.

Jesus said, "Now learn a parable of the fig tree; when his branch is yet tender, and putteth forth leaves, ye know that summer is nigh."[3] In Bible interpretation there is a principle called expositional constancy.

20

Whenever you seek to teach by parable or allegory, certain things remain the same in all the parables or allegories where they're used. If you use a particular symbol for something, it remains symbolic of that thing wherever you find it. For instance, Jesus spoke many parables concerning the field and sowing in the fields. The "field" is an expositional constant. Wherever you read about a field in a parable, or wherever the fields are used in a symbolic sense, you're reading about the world itself. Also, the "seed" is an expositional constant. The seed always refers to the Word of God, which is planted within the world. "Leaven" represents sin. Etc.

The "fig tree" is an expositional constant that always refers in symbolic form to the nation of Israel.

When Jesus was at the Mount of Olives and was hungry, He saw a fig tree and came over to see if it had any fruit. When He got there, there were only leaves on the tree but no fruit. Jesus cursed the tree and immediately it withered and died. The disciples were amazed that it so soon withered and died.[4] In the expositional constant this was a figure of the curse coming upon Israel for their failure to bear fruit. Jesus didn't use His miraculous power to destroy things.

Jeremiah gives a parable of two baskets of figs, one good and one rotten.[5] Jeremiah talks about these rotten figs which have become so spoiled that they have no value at all. The only thing you can do is to get rid of them. The figs are thrown out, and then Jeremiah says that the figs are actually the nation Israel. God is going to disperse them into the world. Yet, Jeremiah said that the Lord will gather them together back in the land again. These spoiled, rotten figs that were to be scattered into the world are going to be brought back again.

When the disciples said, "What shall be the sign of thy coming?"[6] Jesus said, after giving them other signs, "Now learn a parable of the fig tree."[3] I believe that He had Jeremiah's parable in mind.

Now, in the springtime we see the fig trees as they begin to put out their little leaves and we see the first fruits. They have two seasons, actually, and the first ripe figs begin to come out early in the spring. Whenever you see the fig tree begin to leaf out, you know that summer is right around the corner. "Summer is nigh," Jesus said, "So know that my coming is at the door."[7] He's saying that when you see the nation Israel begin to bud forth again, when you see life begin to come into the nation Israel again, you know that His coming is at the doors.

We saw the fig tree begin to bud forth in May of 1948 when it was established again as a nation. And now we see God building up Zion. "When the LORD shall build up Zion, he shall appear in his glory."[2] You're

22

He's Coming Soon — Like Right Away.

watching Zion being built up. Every time you read about it in the newspaper, every time you see an article in the magazines of what's happening in Israel, know this: the Lord is building up Zion. But also know, He's coming in His glory very soon.

In fact, Jesus said, "This generation shall not pass, till all these things be fulfilled."[8] What generation? Not the generation He was talking to—they've passed. The Greek word *genea* used here always refers to that which was immediately preceding. In the Greek it could be translated "that generation." *That generation* which sees the fig tree bud forth, *that generation* which sees the Lord build up Zion shall not pass until all these things—the appearance of the Antichrist, the seven years of tribulation, and the second coming of Christ—be fulfilled. That generation that was living in May of 1948 shall not pass until the second coming of Jesus Christ takes place and the kingdom of God be established upon the earth.

How long is a generation? Forty years on an average in the Bible. Do you remember the children of Israel in the wilderness? They had to be there until that whole generation died. They were wandering 40 years in the wilderness.

Where does that put us? It puts us right out at the end. We're coming down to the wire. The Lord has been waiting, and the

Lord has been giving opportunity to repent and believe in Him. The only reason why Jesus hasn't come already for His Church is because He is so patient and is waiting for the complete fruit of harvest. James said to the Church, "Be patient therefore, brethren, unto the coming of the Lord. Behold, the husbandman waiteth for the precious fruit of the earth, and hath long patience for it."[9] The Lord is only waiting for the complete fruit of the harvest.

I believe at this moment Jesus is standing at the door of heaven just waiting for the signal from the Father. We're that close. Everything that has to be fulfilled has already been fulfilled to bring about this event. Nothing is left in the Scriptures to take place before the rapture of the Church.

Paul said, "Now is our salvation nearer than when we believed . . . let us therefore cast off the works of darkness, and let us put on the armour of light."[10] I believe that the reestablishment of the nation Israel is one of the greatest signs to the world today that the coming of Jesus Christ is even at the doors, and it should be a warning to every child of God.

NOTES

Chapter 3

Signs

It's important to realize that we're talking about the signs of the coming of Jesus Christ, not the signs of the rapture of the Church. There's a difference in time between the rapture of the Church and the second coming of Jesus Christ of approximately seven years (*see* Appendix). When you see the signs of the second coming, you know that the rapture is that much closer.

The disciples asked Jesus: "What shall be the sign of thy coming, and of the end of the world?"[1] Rather than saying, "It's none of your business. You pay attention to your business and I'll pay attention to mine"—He began to tell them the things they could look for that would signal His return to the earth, the things that will happen before He appears again with great glory and power to govern the earth. However, we don't look for all these things to be fulfilled before the Church is caught out.

"This gospel of the kingdom shall be preached in all the world for a witness unto all nations; and then shall the end come."[2] I don't believe that we necessarily will see the gospel preached as a witness by the Church. We're told in Revelation 14 that during the Great Tribulation period the angel of God would be flying through the midst of the heaven declaring the everlasting gospel to all the nations and kindreds and peoples and tribes.[3]

Jesus speaks about the abomination of desolation standing in the holy place as a sign.[4] We as the Church will not see the abomination of desolation. This is strictly Jewish ground. Jesus is talking here to the Jews. This abomination of desolation will not take place until 3½ years into the tribulation period. Then the Antichrist will come to Jerusalem and set up the image of himself within the Holy of Holies of the rebuilt temple. From that point it'll be 1290 days to the coming of Jesus Christ. We can know exactly to the day when Jesus shall come again. We don't know when to start counting yet.

Jesus said that many false Christs and deceivers are going to come—don't follow them.[5] How can you know a false prophet? How can you discern when a man is a false prophet or not? It isn't easy. The most dangerous thing about a false prophet is that 99% of what he tells you is usually true, but

False -dangerous

the 1% area of error is the dangerous part. Let me tell you this. Any man who will cause you to rely for your salvation on any system, any philosophy, any work, any program, or anything other than Jesus Christ and His shed blood for your sins is a false prophet. Though he may tell you 99% truth, if he tries to get you to rely on anything other than Jesus Christ for your eternal life, he's a false prophet.

Jesus said that you'll hear of wars and rumors of wars.[6] Don't be troubled; the end is not yet. Actually, as long as man is on the earth and is so greedy and corrupt, you're going to have wars. Since Jesus made that statement there have been 13 years of war to every one year of peace throughout the history of man. Jesus said that that's not a sign; don't get shook when that begins to happen.

But then He said, "For nation shall rise against nation, and kingdom against kingdom."[7] In the Greek this bespeaks a worldwide state of war. It wasn't until 1914 that we had a worldwide war. Now we've had two. They're talking about World War III and its possibility. World wars *are* a sign that His return is coming close.

Along with these, Jesus said, "There shall be famines."[7] It's amazing how much we're reading of famine in these days. There's the famine in North Africa as a result of the great drought situation. Hundreds of thousands of people are starving to death in

29

Ethiopia and in the northern part of Africa as the Sahara Desert is expanding so rapidly. We really don't know what the answer is. India has had a perennial problem of famine. It has spread to Bangladesh as a result of the recent war. And, of course, China has had the perennial problem.

We've been hearing warnings for a long time that our food production isn't keeping up with the population expansion. There comes a time when the population growth goes beyond the ability of the earth to produce the necessary food. And it seems that we have come very close to that now.

They've been predicting that we'd be having great food shortages here in the United States. When you hear about bombs going off on trains in Italy, it seems so far away. Then one goes off in the airport in L.A.—all of a sudden, it's home. Famines in North Africa seem far away, but we're already experiencing certain food shortages here in the United States. And, as a result, you're paying 72 cents for a loaf of good whole wheat bread.

In addition, the CIA has been studying climate patterns. They say that we're going into a cycle of climate change as took place in the 16th century. There'll be colder winters and shorter growing seasons. Europe won't be able to produce enough food. Canada will no longer produce her abundant wheat crops. The CIA is studying this because it's interested in the security of the United States. And when people start getting hungry, they start looking for supplies. The CIA has estimated that possibly 100 million people will starve in India alone as a result of these climatic changes that are taking place.

Jesus also said that there would be "pestilences."[7] Actually, viruses are sweeping this world today. It seems that whenever science develops an immunization then the viruses develop immunity to the immunizations. They come back next year in a mutated strain, resistant to the medicines that were used last year. So, you get hit all over again with the Asian flu, and type X, or type Z. There are so many types now they can't even name them anymore, they just put numbers or letters on them. Viruses sweeping the world. They can almost predict how many people will have Asian flu in the various parts of the United States this winter.

There's one new virus that's attacking the gums. All of a sudden you think that you have teeth problems because your gums are so sore in the root canals. They hit in different areas of the body. People think that they have appendicitis, but it's a virus. All of a sudden there's a big rash of appendix operations. We don't know how to handle these viruses. And not only viruses, but now we have staph infection plaguing many of our hospitals. Many people survive the operation well, but the staph infection hits them and they actually suffer more with that than they do the initial operation. But the staph infection seems to be impervious to any of the disinfectants they use. There seems to be no way to get rid of it. It's amazing what some of the hospitals have done to get rid of the staph infection, yet it hangs on.

Jesus spoke of "earthquakes, in divers places."[7] The Santa Ana *Register* had an interesting section on earthquakes. It isn't a matter of whether or not we're going to have an earthquake here, it's only a matter of when it's going to happen. They don't even question that we'll have an earthquake. They just don't know when. Orange County has about 5 different fault zones and any of them can give you a good jolt. And the unfortunate part about Orange County is that the water table is so high that any jolt above 6.5 on the Richter scale is apt to "liquefy" the soil so that no building could stand against it. When the earth begins to shake it'll bring all the water to the surface and it'll become one big mud hole. All the buildings would just go into it. And there's nothing they can do.

You may say, "That's sort of bad news, man. I'm reading this to be encouraged." Cheer up! It's going to get worse. I got these facts out of the newspapers and news magazines. I've been watching the documentaries on television. These sad songs and sober things didn't come from me, they came from the news media. These are facts, facts that we need to face. What we're seeing around us in the world today is only a foreshadowing of that which is to come in much greater measure in the Great Tribulation.

David said, "God is our refuge and strength . . . Therefore will not we fear, though the earth be removed, and though the mountains be carried into the midst of the sea."[8] How glorious to put your confidence in the Lord and not in the old earth. Though the mountains be removed and cast into the midst of the sea, because the Lord is my refuge and my strength I will not fear. Whenever an earthquake takes place and things get to shaking around, I say, "Lord, thank you for another sign. Shake 'em, Lord! Let us know Your coming is at hand."

But you say, "Just a minute! We've had wars all the time. And there have been pestilences. You can look at history and find the black plague of Europe and the bubonic plagues. It's nothing new. Famines and earthquakes go back. The city of Philippi was destroyed by an earthquake before Christ. They've been around. How do they constitute signs?"

That's true, they've been around. But not in such intensity and not all together at the same time. It's an interesting fact that recorded earthquakes have increased 200% since the turn of the century. And they're in-

creasing, along with the famines and pestilences, in intensity and the number of people
being struck by them. It's happening during
the same period in which we've had two
world wars. I believe they do constitute
signs—signs of the returning of Jesus Christ.

Now, that shouldn't terrify you and give
you nightmares. In fact, the terrifying thing
would be to think that He wasn't coming
and we'd have to go on in this rotten world
with all the pollution another 10, 15 years.
That to me would really be terrifying. To go
on with the increasing crime and problems
and wars and everything else for another 10
years. Oh, no! That would give me nightmares. But, praise the Lord, it won't be long.
God's plan will be completed and we'll be
taken up!

Days of Noah

After Jesus laid out the many things to
watch for, including the return of the Jews to
Israel and the reestablishing of that nation,
He said, "As the days of Noah were, so shall
also the coming of the son of man be."[9] In
other words, one of the signs of the coming
of Jesus Christ would be that the days would
be like the days of Noah. The sign of the end
of the world would be that the world would
again become as it was before the flood.

What were the days of Noah like? At the
time of Noah there was a population explosion. In those days "men began to multiply
on the face of the earth."[10] Just how many

people there were upon the earth at the time of Noah we don't know. But if the earth's population ratio of increase was the same as it is today, there would've been around 3 billion people at the time of the flood. Almost the same number of people that are upon the earth now.

It's the mathematical formula for population increase that has brought such fear in the hearts of the scientists today. They've projected the average population and growth pattern, and they say that by the year 2000 we're going to have 8 billion people upon the earth. You see, until 1860 there was never (except prior to the flood) more than a billion people upon the earth. The first billion population came by 1860; 2 billion population by 1930; 3 billion population by 1965. The population of the earth is now coming close to the 4 billion mark. At these ratios of increase there will be 8 billion by the turn of the century. But we can't feed the 4 billion we have now.

A second characteristic of the days of Noah was that "God saw that the wickedness of man was great in the earth, and that every imagination of the thoughts of his heart was only evil continually."[11] God saw the wickedness of man. Man's heart and imagination were filled with wickedness continually; evil thoughts constantly filling his mind.

Whenever you who are living in this world

35

today—working in secular positions, going to school, or whatever the case may be—come into contact with the world around you, just listen for a little while to their conversation and stories. What do you discover? You discover that the imagination of man's heart is evil continually. We're living in a very wicked age. Look at the novels that are being written. Look at the movies that are being produced. Better that you not look at them, but consider them. Consider that you can't even send your child to the store to buy a quart of milk but that he's exposed to magazines which, at one time, you couldn't buy unless you bought under the counter. We see that more and more the imagination of man's heart is becoming evil continually.

A third condition that existed upon the earth at the time of Noah was that the earth also was corrupt before God, and the earth was filled with violence. "And God looked upon the earth, and, behold, it was corrupt; for all flesh had corrupted his way upon the earth. And God said unto Noah, The end of all flesh is come before me; for the earth is filled with violence through them; and, behold, I will destroy them with the earth."[12]

When we arrived home from our trip I grabbed my *Time* and *Newsweek* and saw all the violent riots, and read of the crime that is covering the U.S. What's really alarming to the law enforcement officials is the rise of violent crimes in the first six months of the year. The percentage of increase in violent crimes is frightening, but they don't know what to do about it. And one of the terrifying factors is that the majority of violent crimes today are committed by teenagers. It makes you wonder how we can survive another generation. If you'll take the rate of increase of violent crime as it continues to increase year by year, you'll find that soon the entire nation will be so filled with violent crime that you won't be safe *anywhere*.

Now, let me ask you to describe the political scene in one word. If someone asked me, I'd say "corrupt." We see the whole corrupt system. We see the self-interest forces as they're legislating and ruling for their own private interests. We see the corruption, and the corruption leads to the violence. At the time of Noah the earth was corrupt and filled with violence. We see the same thing today.

Psychologists have conducted many interesting experiments with rats to determine certain sociological behavioral patterns. I don't know why they use rats to discover patterns in man, but they do. They observe the behavioral patterns of the rats to try to understand why man behaves as he does. One of the interesting experiments is the placing of more rats in a given area than the area can support. Then they watch the development of antisocial behavioral patterns of these overcrowded rats. The rats begin to be violent with one another. The mothers begin to neglect their children. All kinds of peculiar behavioral patterns develop with these overcrowded rats.

The characteristics that existed at the time of Noah were the multiplying of people upon the face of the earth; and the violence, corruption, and wickedness that began to follow. We see the population explosion today. It could very well be that these are related.

Yet, there's one area here that's interesting statistically. You may blame the urbanization. "I've got to get out of Orange County! I'll flee to some little city in the Midwest. I'll move to the country. We'll move into some small, rural area where we can raise our children, where they can have room to run. They won't be overcrowded. They can hunt and fish and live in a very healthy social environment in the country. We'll take them out of the urban area." But the crimes of violence are increasing far more rapidly in the rural areas than in the urban areas. In fact, the increase in the urban areas is very low; it's the increase in the rural areas that is so high.

Where can you escape the violence? Where can you escape the wickedness? You can't. We went back to the little rural areas of Pennsylvania. You don't get much more rural than some of these boroughs, villages, and townships. We were astounded at the widespread use of drugs by the young people there. It's like it was at its height in the Newport and Huntington Beach areas. Now it's hitting these little rural areas of the U.S. I saw far more kids loaded on drugs in rural Pennsylvania than I've seen around here in a long time. There is no escape. The world is filled with corruption and violence. The imagination of man's heart is evil continually. We see the conditions that existed at the time of Noah existing now as we look around the world in which we live.

Jesus made one further statement and commentary concerning the days of Noah. "For as in the days that were before the flood they were eating and drinking, marrying and giving in marriage, until the day that Noah entered into the ark, and knew not until the flood came."[13] In other words, those people in that generation were totally oblivious to the impending judgment of God which was about to come. "Everything's going to be all right. We'll work it out. Just trust our men of science. They'll come up with a solution." They were totally oblivious to the wrath and the judgment of God which was about to come upon them. Eating, drinking, marrying, giving in marriage—which speaks of business as usual and not aware that they were being ripened for the judgment of God.

As we look around us today, we see a total unconsciousness in the minds and hearts of people of the impending judgment of God which is ready to fall upon this world. Jesus, in warning of these last days, said to "take heed" lest you become ensnared. The snares would be the "cares of this life"—or materialism, drunkenness, and surfeiting—and they will trap many.[14] People will be caught up in a materialistic society. I agree with Billy Graham: "If God doesn't judge the United States, then He owes an apology to Sodom and Gomorrah."

NOTES

_____

_____

_____

_____

_____

_____

_____

_____

_____

_____

_____

_____

_____

_____

_____

Chapter 4

Further Signs

There are events taking place today—which have only happened or begun to happen within our lifetime—that are related to the coming of Jesus Christ and the end of the world.

Daniel the prophet said that in the last days "knowledge shall be increased" and "many shall run to and fro" throughout the entire earth.[1] He speaks of increased knowledge and man's skills developing to the extent that man would be able to travel freely around the world.

This seemed to be totally impractical even a hundred years ago. Just over a hundred years ago that great scientist and Christian, Sir Isaac Watts, made the prediction that one day man would be traveling faster than 25 miles per hour. That prediction was predicated upon Daniel's prophecy that people would be going to and fro throughout the

43

entire earth. Watts theorized that men would have to move faster than the horse and would have to travel about 25 miles per hour in order to move around the world.

At the same time over in France the atheist Voltaire said, "Look what dottering idiots the Bible makes out of otherwise intelligent men. For," he said, "Sir Isaac Watts is now predicting that men will be traveling faster than 25 miles per hour. Any fool knows that if you go faster than that you'll die."

A little over 100 years later we find that Sir Isaac Watts was rather conservative in his prediction and that we, through the modern air transports and so forth, are able to travel to and fro throughout the earth. We see that the men of faith, far from being blind, were men of deep insight. They saw further than other men. Actually, from our vantage point, we can laugh at the folly of the atheist. But this increased knowledge has only happened within our lifetime.

By the same token, Jesus speaks of these last days and the development of technological skills so that man would have the capacity of destroying himself. Jesus said, "Except those days should be shortened, there should no flesh be saved: but for the elect's sake those days shall be shortened."[2] If those days weren't shortened, man could actually wipe himself out. Through the development of nuclear science and atomic warheads, through the arsenal that the United States and Russia have been building, man has now the capacity to destroy himself off the face of the earth. But this has only happened within this last generation. The birth of the atomic age was necessary for the fulfillment of the prophecy of Jesus Christ.

Also, Ezekiel speaks about the latter days when God will bring the Jews back into the land which He had given unto their father Abraham, and that God would gather them together from all the nations of the world. God said that there would be a miracle, a nation would be born in a day.[3] On May 14, 1948 a nation was born in a day and Israel was once again established among the nations of the world. God's Word was fulfilled and the stage was set for the coming of Jesus Christ.

Peter said, "There shall come in the last days scoffers . . . saying, Where is the promise of his coming?" Have you heard people say that? "Talk about the second coming of Jesus Christ! I've heard that before. They've been saying that for years!" Yes, they've been saying it for many years, but just know this—you're that much closer. Scoffers will come and say, "Since the fathers fell asleep, all things continue as they were from the beginning."[4] That's a very good definition of the law of uniformitarianism, which is the basis for the evolutionary theory. All things have continued as they were from the beginning. But Peter said that's not right. He said that "they willingly are ignorant" of the fact that the world was once destroyed by the flood[5] (which is a far more plausible explanation for the fossils and their displacement in the geological column than the evolutionary theory).

Peter also said that "one day is with the Lord as a thousand years, and a thousand years as one day."[6] That's very interesting inasmuch as God said to Hosea that for two days the Jewish people would be cast out, but in the third day God will raise them up again in His sight.[7] For two thousand years they were out of the land but now they're back. We're going into the final period.

In conjunction with Israel becoming a nation again, Zechariah wrote that God would be with them and defend them even though all the nations of the world be gathered together against them.[8] He speaks about them being isolated and alone against the world, and that is the way we find them today. The United States is about the only ally that Israel has. We see that the nations of the world have made their alignment against Israel.

The Love Song sings, "I wouldn't want to be there down Jerusalem way," referring to the time soon when Russia invades Israel according to the prophecy in Ezekiel 38. Knowing the destruction and the desolation that is coming to the Russian army when they invade Israel, knowing that they're going to be so wiped out—I wouldn't want to be there, either. I'll tell you something else. I wouldn't want to be on this earth after Jesus has taken his Church out. Knowing the desolation, knowing the tribulation, knowing the wrath of God that will be revealed from heaven—I wouldn't want to be here to face or to see this wrath of God. More than that, I have no intention of being here!

We also read in Daniel 2 that there will be a confederacy of European nations, ten in all, which will be the final world-ruling power. It's interesting that already there's a federation of European nations known as the Common Market, but at present there are only nine members. However, Greece has made application to join the Common Market. If she's accepted, you'll have the ten nations that Daniel spoke about.

It's during the time of the confederacy of these ten nations that, in Nebuchadnezzar's dream in Daniel, the king saw the rock come out of the mountain not cut with hands. This rock struck the great image of world government (with ten toes) in the feet, and the whole image crumbled. The rock was then established and grew into a mountain that filled the earth—it was a kingdom that shall never end. That rock is Jesus Christ and He is coming to establish the glorious kingdom of God that shall never end. We see man's final world-governing force, which will be headed by Antichrist, developing now. We see its formation in this confederacy of European nations.[9]

It's also interesting that the book of Revelation speaks of a new monetary system in the very last stages of man's development upon the earth. It'll be a monetary system based on assigning an individual number to every person. And no person will be able to buy or sell except he has his number.[10]

Now, this is being talked about in the banking circles already. It's more than just talk, it's in the development and implementing stages. It wasn't possible until the development of the computer. But now, with our computer systems, we realize that the only way our economy can survive is to get rid of money and put everything on a computer. Buying and selling with your assigned number has already been introduced in one of the markets in Santa Ana, which has made arrangements with one of the local savings institutions to issue cards with your assigned number. When you purchase your groceries, your assigned number will be fed into the computer and automatically deduct from your savings the amount of your purchase. The advantage is that you can earn interest on your money up to the time of your purchase.

We see all these things happening right before our eyes. The developments taking place today have made way for these prophecies to be fulfilled.

Also, Revelation speaks about an event taking place in Jerusalem that will be viewed by people around the world.[11] Prior to the development of our telecommunication systems and satellites, claiming that something happening in Jerusalem could be seen here in the United States was sheer folly. But now it's within the realm of possibility for events to be taking place in Jerusalem and for you to be watching them in your living room. Once again, we see how increased knowledge has actually opened the door for all these other things to be fulfilled. Thus, when Jesus said at the end of the book of Revelation, "Behold, I come quickly,"[12] we begin to realize that He was talking to this generation in which we live.

NOTES

Chapter 5

The Tribulation in Perspective

Before the second coming of Jesus Christ, the earth must experience a blood bath. The Scripture tells us that a period of great tribulation is coming to try men who dwell upon the earth. Jesus speaks of it as being a time of tribulation such as the world has never seen before or will ever see again.[1]

Now, the question arises, "Will the rapture precede this Great Tribulation?" There are those who believe that Jesus will come before the tribulation; there are those that say He is coming at the end of the tribulation; others say in the middle. So you have your pre-trib, post-trib, and mid-trib theories. There are arguments and Scriptures that people can present for all these theories. My personal opinion is that Jesus will come before the Great Tribulation to rapture His Church.

Jesus said to the Church, "In the world ye

shall have tribulation."[2] Don't expect an easy route or a bed of roses. He said that if they have rejected Him, they shall reject you—"If they have persecuted me, they will also persecute you" because the servant is not greater than the lord.[3] This tribulation which the Church faces has its origin from Satan, who is still seeking to fight against Jesus Christ. Satan is venting his wrath against Christ by his persecution and tribulation against those who would follow Jesus Christ.

But the Scriptures teach that the Great Tribulation that is coming upon the earth will proceed from God. In Revelation 6 man is calling unto the rocks and the mountains, "Fall on us, and hide us from the face of him that sitteth on the throne, and from the wrath of the Lamb: for the great day of **His** wrath is come; and who shall be able to stand?"[4] The Great Tribulation will actually proceed from God. It starts when Jesus opens this 7-sealed book in heaven; and one of the creatures in heaven says, "Come,"[5] and John sees God's wrath beginning to be poured out upon the earth. We find the Great Tribulation proceeding from God, and even from the throne of God; and we hear the cry from the throne, "Even so, Lord God Almighty, true and righteous are thy judgments,"[6] upon those that dwell upon the earth. So there's a difference in origins for the tribulation the Church faces and the world faces. The tribulation of the Church proceeds from Satan. The Great Tribulation upon the earth proceeds from God.

There's also a difference in those who suffer in the tribulations. Those of the Church that are under the tribulation from Satan are just that—the Church. The object of Satan's tribulation is the Church, whereas the object of the Great Tribulation from God is the Christ-rejecting world. Because they have rejected God's invitations of love, grace, mercy, and truth, the cup of the wrath of His indignation shall overflow upon a Christ-rejecting world, cleansing the world and purifying it for the return of His Son. Thus, though the Church will have tribulation, I don't believe that the Church will go through the Great Tribulation period.

Peter tells us that Lot's righteous soul was vexed by the ungodly living of the people around him, and that God destroyed the cities of Sodom and Gomorrah; but, first of all, He delivered out that righteous man Lot before the destruction came. That was the premise of Abraham to the Lord—Shall not the Judge of the earth do right? Would You destroy the righteous with the wicked?[7] What does the lesson teach? Just this: God will not destroy the righteous with the wicked. "The Lord knoweth how to deliver the godly out of temptations, and to reserve the unjust unto the day of judgment."[8]

Paul said, "For God has not appointed us

to wrath, but to obtain salvation by our Lord Jesus Christ."[9] Paul said the same thing in Romans, "We shall be saved from wrath through him."[10] Jesus, in the whole context of the Great Tribulation, said, "Pray always, that ye may be accounted worthy to escape all these things."[11] You better believe that's what I'm praying! And if you're praying to be accounted worthy to escape all these things and to stand before the Son of God, look for me up there because I'm going to be in that heavenly crowd spoken of in Revelation 5. I'll be up there before the whole thing takes place down here. I hope you'll be there with me! "Unto them that look for him shall he appear the second time."[12]

Are you looking for Christ? Really, that's whom the promise is to—those that are looking for Him. If you have faith that God will take you through the tribulation, watch out, God might honor your faith. Enoch believed God, "and he was not; for God took him."[13] That's the faith I want, like Enoch. I'll be taken up.

In Revelation 1 we find the Lord dividing the book of Revelation into three sections. Jesus said to write: (a) the things which thou hast seen, (b) the things which are, and (c) the things which will be hereafter, which in the Greek is *meta tauta* or, literally, "after these things." John, in obedience to the commandment, wrote in Revelation 1 the vision that he saw of Christ on the Island of Patmos (a). In chapters 2 and 3 he wrote of the things which are—things of the Church and the messages of Jesus unto the seven churches (b). Then, beginning with Revelation 4, John wrote the things which will be after the Church things (c).

Now, there's a portion of the Church that will go into the Great Tribulation. To the church of Thyatira, which had introduced the system of idolatry and worship of idols within the Church, Jesus said: "I have a few things against thee, because thou sufferest that woman Jezebel . . . to teach and to seduce my servants to commit fornication, [that is, spiritual fornication] . . . Behold, I will cast her into a bed, and them that commit adultery with her into great tribulation, except they repent of their deeds."[14]

What part of the Church will go into the Great Tribulation? The church of Thyatira that refuses to repent. The exception was that if the church of Thyatira repented they could escape the Great Tribulation; which would be consistent with the message to the church of Philadelphia where Jesus said, "Because thou hast kept the word of my patience, I also will keep thee from the hour of temptation, which shall come upon all the world, to try them who dwell upon the earth."[15]

Many people who know God and know of Jesus Christ will, no doubt, go into the

Great Tribulation. But the true Church of Christ shall not.

That portion of the Church that refuses to repent, probably including carnal and luke-warm Christians, will be cast into the Great Tribulation. Is that the part of the Church you want to be a part of? Welcome to it. But don't look for me in that number. Because God has promised me something better.

After the close of Jesus' messages to the churches, we've come to the end of Church history. Chapter 4 begins with that Greek phrase *meta tauta*. "After these things," John said, "behold, a door was opened in heaven: and the first voice which I heard was as it were of a trumpet saying unto me, Come up hither, and I will show you things which must be after these things [*meta tauta*]."[16]

As we pointed out, in chapter 1 of Revelation John wrote the things that he *saw*. In chapters 2 and 3 he wrote the things that *are*, the things of Church history. Now, in order that we would not be confused concerning the understanding of this book, the Lord gave us the same Greek phrase, *meta tauta* ("after these things"), twice in chapter 4, verse 1—so that you know you're in the third section of the book: the things that are going to take place *after* the Church history, after the Church is gone, after the Church has completed its ministry upon the earth.

I believe that Revelation 4:1 is the place of

the rapture of the Church. That "voice" in heaven and "trumpet" are the same as in 1 Thessalonians 4:16. With the trump of God, and the archangel saying, "Come up hither," we the Church will be gathered together with the Lord in the heavens when the last one for whom God has been waiting has made his decision for Jesus Christ. The minute he makes his decision, there will be a glorious catching up of the whole body of Christ!

Now, what things are going to happen to this world after the Church history is over? What happens after Revelation 4:1?

John was immediately in the spirit, this spiritual timeless dimension. I believe that John actually beheld these things that he writes about. He actually saw them as though they were happening right then. He went into this time chamber, so to speak. He said in chapter 1, "I was in the Spirit unto the day of the Lord."[17] Thus, he was able to see these things as though they were happening then, even though it would be another two thousand years before they would transpire.

John continues to describe the heavenly scene in the remainder of chapter 4. In chapter 5 he saw the scroll with seven seals in the right hand of Him Who is sitting upon the throne. An angel proclaimed with a loud voice, "Who is worthy to open the scroll and to loose the seals?" John began to sob convulsively because no one in heaven, nor earth, nor under the earth was found worthy to even look upon the scroll.[18]

Then one of the elders said, "Weep not: behold, the Lion of the tribe of Judah, the Root of David, hath prevailed to open the scroll, and to loose the seals." And John turned and saw Him as a Lamb that had been slain, "and He came and took the scroll out of the right hand of him that sat upon the throne."[19]

Immediately, the 24 elders brought forth the "vials full of odors, which are the prayers of saints. And they sang a new song, saying, Thou art worthy to take the scroll, and to open the seals thereof: for thou wast slain, and hast redeemed us to God by thy blood out of every kindred, and tongue, and people, and nation; and hast made us unto our God kings and priests: and we shall reign [with Him] on the earth."[20]

Notice the lyrics of the song that's being sung. Who can sing that song? It's not the song of Israel and the covenant relationship with God, because it's people from all the families of the earth, not just the one family of Abraham. It's a people who have been redeemed by the blood of Jesus Christ. Only the Church can sing that song. I don't know the tune yet, but I've got the lyrics memorized!

When Jesus takes the scroll, you find innumerable multitudes, millions upon millions, worshiping the Lamb and declaring His worthiness to receive the honor, and the authority, and the glory. Jesus proceeds to loose the seals of the scrolls in Revelation 6. With the very first seal there comes forth the white horse rider going forth conquering and to conquer which, I believe, is the entrance of the Antichrist, because it's followed by wars and death and famine and desolation. Certainly, the second coming of Christ won't be followed by such events but by the glorious establishment of the kingdom. Actually, Revelation chapters 6 through 19 describe the events that are happening upon the earth when God's judgment and wrath are being poured out upon the Christ-rejecting world. God is cleansing the world and purifying it for the return of His Son.

Now, where's the Church? Before the tribulation ever begins it's in heaven singing and praising the Lord for His worthiness to take the scroll and loose the seals. The Great Tribulation doesn't start until the seals are broken.

Jesus, when talking about His second coming, said, "Immediately after the tribulation of those days . . . they shall see the Son of man coming in the clouds of heaven with power and great glory."[21] This "cloud" is the Church that is coming with Him. Do you remember in the 12th chapter of Hebrews—after chapter 11, the great chapter of faith and all these men of faith are listed—it said, "seeing we also are compassed about with so great a cloud of witnesses . . . let us run with patience the race that is set before us."[22] The Church, or the people of God, are many times referred to as a "cloud."

Why, then, is there all the confusion concerning post-tribulation, mid-trib, and pre-trib rapture? In chapter 13 of the book of Revelation there's a reference to the beast (Antichrist) making war against the saints, and he's given power "to overcome them" during the middle of the tribulation period.[23]

Those that are proclaiming that the Church will go through the Great Tribulation are proclaiming a super-church—a church super-endowed with spiritual gifts, to be manifested as the sons of God before the world. They claim that this super-church will actually bring to pass the kingdom of Christ upon the earth, for they shall manifest all the powers of Christ. But notice that the beast shall "overcome them."

It is impossible that the power of the Antichrist could overcome the Church. As Jesus said, "The gates of hell shall not prevail against it."[24] Therefore, I reject these "saints" as being the Church. This is actually a reference to the nation Israel which God shall be dealing with throughout this seven-year period, "the time of Jacob's trouble."[25] The Jews are the headliners at this time as far as God's program is concerned. The "saints" referred to here are of the nation Israel—the Church having already been delivered.

Then Jesus shall "gather together his elect from the four winds."[26] By defining "His elect" as being the Church, you'd have the Church in the tribulation period. But I believe that "His elect" is a reference to the nation Israel if you read it in context. Jesus said, "Pray ye that your flight be not in the winter, neither on the sabbath day" when fleeing out of Jerusalem.[27] How many of you in the Church expect to be in Jerusalem fleeing when the Antichrist sets up his image within the temple? How many of you would be praying, "O God, don't let it be on the Sabbath day"? Why are you worried about the Sabbath day? The Church doesn't keep the Sabbath day. Actually, the Church celebrates the Lord's day which, I'm fully persuaded, is *every* day. But how many of you won't travel more than two-thirds of a mile on Saturday? That's God's covenant relation with Israel.[28] The "elect" refers to the nation Israel. Jesus will gather them back into the land for the kingdom age at His return.

I believe the confusion arises because people don't see the prophecies of God's dealing with the restoration of the nation Israel—establishing them in a priority basis

63

again upon the earth and bestowing His favor upon them.

Paul said in Romans 11, "that blindness in part is happened to Israel, until the fulness of the Gentiles be come in."[29] In this interim time when Israel has been forsaken, God did speak of His going forth unto the Gentiles and of the gospel being preached to them. He would be called God by a people, the Gentiles, who didn't know Him. So, we've been in this time of the Church, the time of the Gentiles, in which the message of Jesus Christ has come to us and the hope of God has filled our hearts. But the time of the Gentiles is just about over.

Paul continued in Romans 11, then "all Israel shall be saved: as it is written, There shall come out of Zion the Deliverer, and shall turn away ungodliness from Jacob."[30] I believe very definitely that the mistakes and the confusion arise out of a misunderstanding of God's dealing with the nation Israel; they'll be going through the Great Tribulation. This'll be the time when, as even Jesus said, "Ye shall not see me henceforth, till you shall say, Blessed is he that cometh in the name of the Lord."[31] After the Great Tribulation period Israel will be saying, "O, blessed is He Who comes in the name of the Lord!" Zechariah the prophet said, "And one shall say unto him, What are these wounds in thine hands? Then he shall answer, Those which I received in the house

64

of my friends."[32] Thus, the glorious first recognition of Jesus Christ as Israel's Messiah when He comes the second time with the Church to establish His reign upon the earth.

Confusion also arises because of the attempt to equate the "last trump" of 1 Corinthians[33] at the rapture with the "seventh trumpet" of the book of Revelation[34] near the end of the Great Tribulation. But the last trump referred to in Corinthians is actually a military allusion. It's that trumpet call given as a signal to gather troops together or to cause the troops to advance. There's an absence of the definite article which would preclude a reference to the seventh trumpet of the book of Revelation in corresponding Greek grammar. The last trump would need to have the article (which is absent) and, thus, it could not refer to the seventh trumpet. (See *Greek New Testament* by Henry Alford.) As John said, the last trump will say to the Church, "Come up hither!"[35]

Jesus said that some would come and say that the "Lord delayeth his coming." But in Matthew 24 He said, "That evil servant shall say in his heart, My Lord delayeth his coming."[36] Anyone who would proclaim to you that "the Lord delayeth his coming" isn't really a righteous servant of God but is, indeed, an evil servant. For those are evil tidings that do not, as they proclaim, create a righteous motivation within the Church. The theory or the philosophy that the Lord delayeth His coming, rather than tending toward righteousness, tends toward slothfulness, according to Jesus Christ.

It's the imminent coming of Jesus Christ that tends toward holiness, righteous living, and purity. John says, "Every man that hath this hope in him purifieth himself, even as he is pure."[37] What hope? The hope that at any moment the Lord is going to appear. Jesus is going to change me, and I'll be just like Him. I'll have a new body just like His. This corruption will go through a metamorphosis and I'll receive my new body like that of Jesus Christ. The greatest purifying influence within the Church today is the imminent return of Jesus Christ.

Actually, the doctrine of the "Lord delayeth his coming" is a damnable doctrine. I'd be very careful about any doctrine proclaiming that the "Lord delayeth his coming," for the effect of it is diabolic. It causes you to believe that you have to go through the Great Tribulation and see the Antichrist. The effect is that you're no longer looking for Jesus Christ—you're looking for the Antichrist. Your whole attention is directed to waiting for this man of sin to be revealed because you now think this is necessary before Christ comes.

Secondly, this doctrine would have you prepare for the Great Tribulation rather than to meet the Lord. You'd find yourself in all kinds of preparation to survive the tribulation—storing all kinds of food so you could eat without taking the mark of the beast, etc.

How insidious is this doctrine that declares the "Lord delayeth his coming." For, in reality, there isn't one single prophecy left that needs to be fulfilled before the rapture of the Church. Everything that has been prophesied has already been fulfilled in regard to the catching up of the Church. The unfulfilled prophecies remain for that period *after* the Church is "caught up." We are at the very door—nothing is left. The next great event of the Church will be the catching up to be with the Lord. It could happen this very hour!

NOTES

Chapter 6

What Should I Do?

In light of the fact that the Lord might come even today, what should you do as a Christian?

First, let me tell you what you shouldn't do. You shouldn't quit your job, sell your house, or see how much money you can borrow figuring you wouldn't have to pay it back. Jesus said, "Occupy till I come."[1] He intends for us to go right on. Waiting for Him—yes. Watching for Him. But also continuing in our occupations and in our work.

After Paul had written his first letter to the Thessalonians, they thought: "Wow! The Lord's coming right away! Let's all quit our jobs and just sit around and wait for Him to come." So, Paul quickly wrote to them the second letter saying, "Go back to work! You didn't understand what I was telling you. You're not to quit your job. If you don't work, you shouldn't eat."[2] Paul told them to get back to work, that they'd taken the wrong attitude in light of the return of the Lord.

Jesus said, "Watch."[3] As a Christian you should be watching. "And unto them that look for him shall he appear the second time."[4]

Secondly, you should be ready. Jesus said, "Therefore be ye also ready: for in such an hour as you think not the Son of man cometh."[5] Jesus gave us some parables concerning readiness. He said that the lord went away and left his goods in the hands of his servant. But the servant began to get drunk and to sluff off, and the lord came back when the servant wasn't expecting him.[6]

Amos cried out, "Prepare to meet thy God."[7] You need to prepare. That preparation is in giving your heart and life to Jesus Christ, and receiving His forgiveness and the blotting out of your sins and transgressions. And then wait. James said, "Be patient therefore, brethren, unto the coming of the Lord. Behold, the husbandman is waiting . . . be ye also patient; establish your hearts."[8]

Peter tells us that in the last days scoffers would come and say, "Where's the promise of His coming? They've been saying that for years. My grandmother used to sit around and talk about the second coming!" But the Bible said, "The Lord is not slack concerning his promise, as some men count slackness; but is longsuffering to us." Then Peter said, giving the reason for the delay, that God is "not willing that any should perish, but that all should come to repentance."[9]

Now, I realize that many times there's a hesitancy in our hearts when we think of the coming of Christ. Jesus said to John at the end of the Revelation, "Surely I come quickly." John said, "Even so, come, Lord Jesus." When I think of the coming of the Lord, my heart responds, "Even so, come quickly, Lord Jesus!"

A young man came up to me and said: "You know, I can't pray that. It hurts me when people pray that, because there are so many in my family who aren't yet saved. And I think if the Lord would come, they'd be lost."

Now, I don't think they will necessarily be lost. I believe the Scriptures teach that a great multitude of people will be saved out of the Great Tribulation. In Revelation 7 John saw a great multitude in heaven which no man could number out of all the nations and kindreds. They wore white robes and were singing of salvation. The elder said to John, "Who are they? Where'd they come from?" John said, "Thou knowest." And the elder said, "These are they which came up out of the great tribulation, and have washed their robes, and made them white in the blood of the Lamb."[10] In chapter 6 under the fifth seal, those souls that were martyred during the tribulation period are waiting for their opportunity to enter the heavenly scene. They're told to wait a little longer until the total number is martyred as they were martyred.[11] Then they could come into the heavenly scene. I believe that in chapter 7 we see those martyred during the tribulation period coming into the heavenly scene.

But that's a hard way to come. Why wait? Why sluff off your chances of joining in the glorious excitement of being with the Lord when He catches up the Church? Why say, "I'll wait until the tribulation comes and then I'll die for Christ"? If you can't live for Christ now, how in the world are you going to die for Him then? How much better to go with the Church than to be left behind and face the Great Tribulation and all that horror that's coming upon the earth. Why make it tough on yourself when the Lord wants to make it easy on you? Why not just open your heart and life to Jesus Christ now? Why not just receive Him as your Lord and Saviour and, as He said, be ready? What you need to be ready is Jesus Christ dwelling in your heart and in your life.

I believe that many of our loved ones who've been hassled by our witness and by our testimony and have been upset—once we've disappeared, they're going to say, "Hey! They knew what they were talking about!" I believe that there'll be multitudes who will be saved during the tribulation period.

Now, if suddenly today the whole Church left and you were still sitting here, you know that you'd think twice about the Lord. And so, many will realize, once the Church is taken out, that they've actually missed the opportunity of being raptured with the Church. But, I believe, they'll become dead serious with God and will be martyred during the Great Tribulation by refusing to take the mark of the beast. They'll take death in preference to the mark and, thus, will be saved. But it's a hard way to go. And there's no reason to go that way when the Lord has provided the better way through Jesus Christ today.

I think the question at this point is, "Are *you* ready?" Should the Lord call it quits today and say: "This is the end for the Church. You've finished your witness. Come home!"—where would you be? Would you be gathered with the Church and with the Lord in the air? Or would you be down here scratching your head wondering what's going on?

There's no sense in being lost when Jesus has made provision for your salvation. It doesn't make sense to go on in sin when you can be cleansed, to go on in darkness when you can walk in the light, to go on in bitterness and hatred when you can experi-

75

ence His love. You can know peace with God by just submitting and surrendering yourself to Jesus Christ.

A NEW LIFE!

We trust that the Holy Spirit has spoken to you as you have read this book. We believe these are the last days and that Jesus is coming soon. The important thing is to be ready for Him when the rapture of all true believers occurs.

Jesus said, "I am the way, the truth, and the life. No man can come unto the Father but by Me" (John 14:6).

The Bible says, "All have sinned and fall short of the glory of God" (Rom. 3:23). "But God demonstrated His own love toward us in that, while we were yet sinners, Christ died for us" (Rom. 5:8). "For God so loved the world that He gave His only begotten Son, that whosoever believes in Him should not perish but have everlasting life" (John 3:16).

Receive Jesus Christ into your life today. Ask Him to forgive you of all your sins, and make Him the Lord of your life. May the Lord richly bless you with your new life in Jesus Christ.

APPENDIX

Many question why we assert that the tribulation period will last seven years when this is not stated specifically in the Bible.

In Daniel 9 the angel told the prophet that 70 seven's were determined on the nation Israel "to finish the transgression, and to make an end of sins, and to make reconciliation for iniquity"—which Jesus did in His first coming. But Daniel went on to say, "to bring in everlasting righteousness, and to seal up the vision and prophecy, and to anoint the most Holy" One—which hasn't happened yet, but will happen at the second coming of Christ.

From the time the commandment went forth to restore and rebuild Jerusalem unto the Messiah the Prince was to be 7 seven's and 62 seven's, or 69 seven-year periods, or 483 years (Dan. 9:25). Because the Babylonian calendar was based on a 360-day year, that would be 173,880 days. We know that Artaxerxes gave the commandment to restore and rebuild Jerusalem on March 14, 445 B.C.—173,880 days later would come to April 6, 32 A.D., the very Sunday that Christ made His triumphant entry into Jerusalem. And according to the prophecy, the Messiah, rather than receiving His kingdom, was cut off for the people (Dan. 9:26).

Inasmuch as the 69 seven's proved to be

seven-year periods, it's reasonable to assume that the seventieth "seven" will also be a seven-year period. So, before Jesus comes there must be one more seven-year period when God deals with the nation Israel once again. This will begin after the fullness of the Gentiles be come in and the Church is gone. God's time clock has been stopped during the Church age.

The Antichrist will make a covenant with Israel, which he'll break in the middle of the seven-year period, and he'll set up the abomination that causes desolation in the Holy of Holies of the rebuilt temple. He'll also cause the daily oblations and sacrifices to cease—1290 days later the Messiah will come the second time and bring in everlasting righteousness. Jesus will "seal up" or complete the visions and prophecies and will be anointed for His reign as King of Kings and Lord of Lords.

FOOTNOTES

Chapter 1
1. 1 Thessalonians 4:16, 17
2. Jude 14
3. Colossians 3:4
4. 1 Thessalonians 4:17
5. 1 Corinthians 15:51, 52
6. 1 John 3:2
7. Philippians 3:20, 21
8. 1 Corinthians 15:53
9. v. 49
10. Matthew 24:36
11. Daniel 12:11
12. Matthew 24:37
13. Luke 17:34-36
14. 1 Thessalonians 5:1-4
15. John 3:7
16. v. 14, 15
17. v. 16

Chapter 2
1. Ezekiel 38:8, 16
2. Psalms 102:16
3. Matthew 24:32
4. Matthew 21:19, 20
5. Jeremiah 24:1, 2
6. Matthew 24:3
7. vv. 32, 33
8. v. 34
9. James 5:7
10. Romans 13:11, 12

Chapter 3
1. Matthew 24:3
2. v. 14
3. Revelation 14:6
4. Matthew 24:15
5. v. 5
6. v. 6
7. v. 7
8. Psalms 46:1, 2
9. Matthew 24:37
10. Genesis 6:1
11. v. 5
12. vv. 12, 13
13. Matthew 24:38, 39
14. Luke 21:34, 35

Chapter 4
1. Daniel 12:4
2. Matthew 24:22
3. Isaiah 66:7-9
4. 2 Peter 3:3, 4
5. vv. 5, 6
6. v. 8
7. Hosea 6:2
8. Zechariah 12:1-9
9. Daniel 2:31-45
10. Revelation 13:16-18
11. Revelation 11:9
12. Revelation 22:7

Chapter 5

1. Matthew 24:21
2. John 16:33
3. John 15:20
4. Revelation 6:16, 17
5. v. 1
6. Revelation 16:7
7. Genesis 18:23, 25
8. 2 Peter 2:6-9
9. 1 Thessalonians 5:9
10. Romans 5:9
11. Luke 21:36
12. Hebrews 9:28
13. Genesis 5:22-24, Hebrews 11:5
14. Revelation 2:20-22
15. Revelation 3:10
16. Revelation 4:1
17. Revelation 1:10
18. Revelation 5:2-4
19. vv. 5-7
20. vv. 8-10
21. Matthew 24:29, 30
22. Hebrews 12:1
23. Revelation 13:7
24. Matthew 16:18
25. Jeremiah 30:7
26. Matthew 24:31
27. v. 20
28. Exodus 31:17
29. Romans 11:25
30. v. 26
31. Matthew 23:39
32. Zechariah 13:6
33. 1 Corinthians 15:52
34. Revelation 8:2, 11:15
35. Revelation 4:1
36. Matthew 24:48
37. 1 John 3:3

Chapter 6

1. Luke 19:13
2. 2 Thessalonians 3:10
3. Matthew 24:42
4. Hebrews 9:28
5. Matthew 24:44
6. vv. 45-51
7. Amos 4:12
8. James 5:7, 8
9. 2 Peter 3:3-9
10. Revelation 7:9-14
11. Revelation 6:9-11